Write On...
SPACE

Clare Hibbert

W
FRANKLIN WATTS
LONDON • SYDNEY

Franklin Watts
First published in Great Britain in 2016 by The Watts Publishing Group

Credits
Series Editor: Melanie Palmer
Conceived and produced by Hollow Pond
Editor: Clare Hibbert @ Hollow Pond
Designer: Amy McSimpson @ Hollow Pond
Illustrations: Kate Sheppard
Photographs: Alamy: 6–7 (Science Photo Library), 26–27 (Purestock);
NASA: 21, 25, 29; Shutterstock: cover (NASA/Vadim Sadovski), 4–5
(Pavel Tvrdy), 9 (Fotovadrat), 11 (Catmando), 12–13 (NASA/Vadim
Sadovski), 15 (Mclek), 17 (esfera), 19 (KPG_Payless), 23 (Vasily
Smirnov), 29 background (Mikhail Grachikov).
Every attempt has been made to clear copyright. Should there be any
inadvertent omission please apply to the publisher for rectification.

ISBN 978 1 4451 5016 1

Printed in China

FSC
www.fsc.org
MIX
Paper from
responsible sources
FSC® C104740

Franklin Watts
An imprint of
Hachette Children's Group
Part of The Watts Publishing Group
Carmelite House
50 Victoria Embankment
London EC4Y 0DZ

An Hachette UK Company
www.hachette.co.uk

www.franklinwatts.co.uk

Look out for the **Write On...** writing tips and tools
scattered through the book, then head to the Writing school on
page 28 for project ideas to inspire your awesome inner author.

Write On... SPACE

CONTENTS

Stargazing

People have gazed up in wonder at the sky for thousands of years. On a clear night, you can see stars, some planets and Earth's Moon – you don't even need a telescope.

Ancient peoples studied the stars. They noticed that some groups of bright stars seem to form a pattern or a picture. They made up names for these constellations that we still use today, such as Leo the Lion and Perseus.

A closer look

About 400 years ago, the Italian astronomer Galileo used the newly invented telescope to get a better view of space. These days our observatories – buildings for viewing the sky – house powerful telescopes. Our knowledge of the Universe is growing all the time.

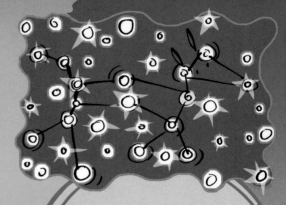

The brightest star in the night sky is Sirius, also known as the dog star. It is part of a constellation called the Great Dog.

It's not just the night sky that tells us about space. During the day we can see the star that's nearest to us – the Sun!

Observatories are built far from lit-up towns and cities, where there is the clearest view.

Write On...

The constellation Perseus is named after a Greek hero. Make up a hero that you could name a star after. What amazing exploits does he or she have?

The Universe

Our planet Earth is just one tiny speck in the Universe. The Universe is the name for everything there is – planets, stars and galaxies. It's so big that astronomers haven't managed to see all of it yet.

The Universe was born about 15 billion years ago in an enormous explosion called the Big Bang. Before that, everything in it was packed together in one small lump. The Big Bang made the Universe grow outwards at great speed.

Where will it all end?
Some scientists think the Universe will keep getting bigger forever. Others believe that one day it might collapse in on itself and come to an end with the Big Crunch!

Most of the Universe is made up of mysterious stuff we can't see. Scientists call this dark matter and dark energy.

Write On...

Remember dark matter and dark energy when you next write a mystery story. Don't make everything obvious. For the reader, not quite seeing the whole picture will add to the spookiness.

The Big Bang might have looked like this.

Stars and galaxies

From here on Earth, stars (except the Sun) look like twinkling white dots. Up close, they are big burning balls of gas, giving off heat and light. They appear to twinkle because Earth's atmosphere bends some of their light as it travels towards us.

 Our neighbouring galaxy, M31, is better known as Andromeda. It is named after a princess in Greek mythology.

 Shooting stars aren't stars at all. They are lumps of space rock, blazing across the sky as they burn up in Earth's atmosphere.

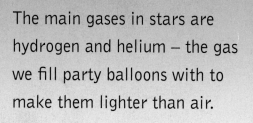 The main gases in stars are hydrogen and helium – the gas we fill party balloons with to make them lighter than air.

Groups of stars are called galaxies. There are about a hundred billion galaxies. They can be spiral-shaped, elliptical (oval) or irregular (no particular shape).

Write On...

Use a thesaurus to help build up a treasure chest of alternative verbs for stars. How about **shine**, **twinkle**, **blaze**, **sparkle** and **glint**?

This milky-white trail across the night sky is made up of stars from our galaxy.

Our galaxy, the Milky Way, is a spiral-shaped galaxy.

Star life and death

Stars are born in huge spinning clouds of gas and dust. They live for as long as they have gas to burn – for millions or billions of years.

The Sun is a medium-sized star. It was born 4.6 billion years ago and will start to die in 5 billion years' time. First it will swell into a red giant, 150 times bigger than it is now. Once it has used up all its gas fuel it will shrink into a white dwarf. When it finally cools, it will be a black dwarf.

Supergiants and supernovas

Massive stars die differently. They swell into supergiants, a million times bigger than the Sun. Supergiants die in a spectacular explosion called a supernova. They leave behind a neutron star – a star that is very small but very dense (it has a big mass for its size).

Neutron stars are only about 10 km across – the same size as a city – but their mass is 1.4 times that of the Sun!

The most massive stars collapse in on themselves when they die and form a black hole. Nothing can escape the pull of a black hole's gravity – not even light.

The clouds of gas and dust where stars are born are called nebulas. This is the Eagle Nebula.

Write On...

Try writing an exciting story about a spacecraft that narrowly misses being pulled into a black hole. Or, if you prefer, write about disappearing into one – and what exists on the other side.

The Solar System

'Solar' means to do with our star, the Sun. The Solar System is made up of the Sun and all the planets and other space bodies that are orbiting (going around) it.

Eight planets orbit the Sun. From closest to furthest away they are: Mercury, Venus, Earth, Mars, Jupiter, Saturn, Uranus and Neptune. Scientists believe there must be a ninth planet, too, because of the way other faraway objects are moving – they must be being pulled by its gravity.

Pluto was counted as the ninth planet until 2006, when scientists decided it was a dwarf planet instead.

Dirty snowballs

Comets are dirty snowballs that are travelling around the Sun. They have an icy centre surrounded by a cloud of gas and dust. Most comets stay out on the edge of the Solar System. Ones that come near to the Sun grow tails of gas and dust.

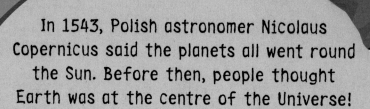

In 1543, Polish astronomer Nicolaus Copernicus said the planets all went round the Sun. Before then, people thought Earth was at the centre of the Universe!

Write On...

Earth

Mars

Jupiter

Sun

Mercury

Venus

Neptune

Saturn

Uranus

13

Our planet

Earth is special. It is the only planet known to support life. More than ten million species live on Earth. Life is possible because of heat and light from the Sun.

As it orbits the Sun, Earth also spins on its axis. One turn takes 24 hours. During this time, we have day and night as we face and then turn away from the Sun.

It takes one full year for Earth to orbit the Sun. Earth is tilted, so while one half is angled towards the Sun, the other is angled away from it. That's why we have seasons — when the northern half has summer, the southern half has winter.

Path of Earth's orbit

Sun

Top half of Earth has summer

Moments of darkness

During a solar eclipse, the Moon passes between the Sun and the Earth. It blocks out the Sun.

NEVER LOOK DIRECTLY AT THE SUN, EVEN DURING AN ECLIPSE. WEAR SPECIAL SAFETY GLASSES.

Write On...

Write a news story about a solar eclipse. Remember to include key facts, such as **when** and **where** it happened. Think of a snappy headline to draw in the reader.

Water covers about 70 per cent of Earth. No wonder it is nicknamed the Blue Planet.

Rocky worlds

The four planets closest to the Sun are called the terrestrial (rocky) planets. They are Mercury, Venus, Earth and Mars. Earth is the biggest of the rocky planets.

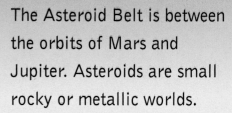

 Mercury is the smallest planet in the Solar System.

 The Asteroid Belt is between the orbits of Mars and Jupiter. Asteroids are small rocky or metallic worlds.

 Mars used to have oceans – and if there was water, there may have been life. Mars still has some water, mostly frozen at its poles.

 Even though Mercury is closer to the Sun, Venus is the hottest planet. It has thick clouds that hold in the heat and is eight times hotter than the Sahara.

 A Mercury day (how long it takes to spin on its axis) is twice as long as a Mercury year (how long it takes to orbit the Sun).

Write On...

Lots of stories tell of alien life on Mars. Imagine what Martians might look like, and come up with some adjectives to describe them.

Mars is known as the Red Planet. Its surface contains lots of iron oxide – the same stuff that makes blood red.

Gas giants

Jupiter   Saturn

Neptune

Uranus

The next four planets away from the Sun are Jupiter, Saturn, Uranus and Neptune. They are called the gas giants, because they are mostly made up of gas. They are much bigger than the planets near the Sun.

Jupiter is so huge that all the other planets could fit inside it twice with room to spare! The Great Red Spot on its surface is a storm that has been raging for more than 300 years.

Spinning rings

Saturn is famous for its beautiful rings. It has thousands of them, organised into bands. Saturn's rings are bright because they are made of ice. The other gas giants have rings, too, but they are darker. Jupiter has four rings, Uranus has thirteen and Neptune has five.

Jupiter, Saturn and Neptune are named after Roman gods. Uranus is named after the Greek god of the sky.

Uranus's rings seem to go from top to bottom. They are really around its middle – it's just that the planet was knocked on to its side billions of years ago.

The first person to see Saturn's rings was the Italian scientist Galileo in 1610.

Write On...

Make a Saturn-shaped poem! Draw Saturn on a piece of lined paper and cut it out. Write a poem about the planet on it, changing the lengths of the lines to fit the space.

Many moons

Moons are rocky bodies that orbit planets. Mercury and Venus don't have moons, but all the other planets do. We have one, Mars has two and the gas planets have dozens each!

Jupiter wins the prize for the most moons. It has 63 of them! Saturn comes a close second with 62 moons. Ganymede, which orbits Jupiter, is the biggest moon in our Solar System.

Earth's Moon

Our Moon seems to shine, but really it is reflecting the Sun's light. It takes about a month for the Moon to orbit the Earth. During this time, its appearance changes from New Moon (not visible on Earth) to Full Moon and back again.

Most moons are round, but not the two orbiting Mars. Deimos and Phobos look like lumpy old potatoes!

Moon in Earth's shadow

Earth between Sun (not shown) and Moon

During a lunar eclipse, the Earth comes between the Sun and Moon, blocking out its light.

Half Moon

New Moon

Full Moon

Half Moon

Write On...

How many songs can you think of that are about the Moon or the stars? Try and write some lyrics (rhyming lines for a song) that have a space theme.

Astronaut Buzz Aldrin on the Moon in July 1969 (see page 24)

Rocket power

The first rocket in space was a V2, a weapon invented in the Second World War (1939–1945). In 1957, a rocket transported the first satellite into space.

The first reusable rocket was the space shuttle. Shuttles flew 135 space missions between 1981 and 2011.

We still use rockets to put satellites into orbit around the Earth. Satellites do many jobs for us, including passing on TV and phone signals. We also use rockets to transport spacecraft, astronauts and space station supplies.

Lift off!

Rockets have to go extremely fast to escape the pull of Earth's gravity – at least 7.9 km/s. This takes a lot of fuel. Rockets are made up of two or three parts, called stages. Each stage is just a huge fuel tank and engine. It falls away from the rest of the rocket when its fuel is used up.

Write On...

An onomatopoeia (say *o-no-mat-o-pee-a*) is a word that sounds like its meaning. Think of examples that describe a rocket taking off, such as **kaboom**, **rumble**, **roar** and **whoosh**.

The Moon is about 384,400 km away. It takes about 13 hours to reach it by rocket.

This rocket is taking off from a launch pad in Kazakhstan.

23

People in space

It takes years of study and work to become an astronaut. You have to be good at science or engineering. Astronauts carry out experiments on the space station or fix telescopes and other objects up in space.

 The first person in space was Russia's Yuri Gagarin. He orbited Earth in his Vostok spacecraft in April 1961.

 It's tricky living on a space station – there's no gravity, so everything floats around!

 The first people to walk on the Moon were the Americans Neil Armstrong and Buzz Aldrin in July 1969 (see page 21).

 The Moon is the only other world astronauts have visited – yet! There are plans to put people on Mars within 20 years.

 The International Space Station (ISS) has been crewed since 2000. It's the ninth space station to be built in space.

American astronaut Karen Nyberg has fun in zero gravity on the ISS!

Write On...

Try writing a short story using two voices or points of view. Try describing the feelings of two astronauts, one fearful and one excited. Make each voice different and unique.

Probes and rovers

Many space missions don't involve astronauts at all. Uncrewed missions are made by space probes; robotic craft with onboard computers. Probes can explore places where humans can't go.

Some probes land on other worlds. The Spirit and Opportunity rovers landed on Mars in 2004. We lost contact with Spirit in 2010, but Opportunity is still working. It studies rocks and soil.

Flybys

Probes also gather information by flying close to other planets or moons. There have been flybys past all eight planets. The Cassini probe has been orbiting Saturn since 2004. It also landed a smaller probe on Saturn's moon Titan, sending back amazing images of its landscape.

The New Horizons probe flew past Jupiter in 2007 and the dwarf planet Pluto in 2015. It is the same size as a baby grand piano.

Voyager 1 left our Solar System in 2012 and is the farthest probe from Earth. It carries a message in case it's ever found by aliens!

Opportunity rover uses antennas to radio its findings back to Earth.

Write On...

Comparisons improve your descriptions. Ones that use **as** or **like** (eg. **the same size as**) – are similes. Ones that don't (e.g. **dwarf planet**) are metaphors. Come up with some of your own.

Write On... Writing school

Are you ready to show off some of the terrific space facts you've found out? First, decide on your form. Here are some ideas:

 A speech you would make if you were chosen to be one of the first people on Mars.

 A short film script about a spacecraft's onboard computer developing a mind of its own. What happens to the astronauts?

 A poem that describes the first – or last – few moments of the Universe.

 If you like drawing, you can always tell a story through a comic strip, like the one below about the space shuttle.

THE SHUTTLE WAS THE FIRST REUSABLE SPACECRAFT. IT TOOK OFF FROM THE KENNEDY SPACE CENTER IN FLORIDA, USA, LIKE A ROCKET, BUT IT LANDED LIKE A PLANE.

TWO SHUTTLE MISSIONS ENDED IN DISASTER: CHALLENGER IN 1986 AND COLUMBIA IN 2003. IN EACH CASE, ALL SEVEN CREW WERE LOST.

THE LAST SHUTTLE TAKE-OFF WAS ON 8 JULY 2011. ATLANTIS DELIVERED SUPPLIES TO THE ISS THEN RETURNED TO EARTH. THE WHOLE FLIGHT LASTED JUST 91 MINUTES.

Imagine being up on the International Space Station.
Write a diary of how you feel and what you see.

ASTRONAUT'S DIARY

It's very strange looking down on the Earth from up here. Space is so big ... and our planet is so beautiful. One of the strangest things is that there's no noise here. It's hard to imagine all the sounds and bustling of life on Earth from this great distance.

One of the big surprises was seeing how the Earth spins on its axis and how different parts of the world have day and night. Because I'm orbiting the Earth, I get to see super-fast sunrises and sunsets, each only seconds long.

I'm so busy that I don't have time to be homesick! It's such a privilege to be up here – I'm treasuring every moment.

My view
of Earth
from the ISS

Why not make up tweets about being in space?
Each tweet can only be 140 characters long.

Glossary

antenna An aerial that sends or receives radio signals.

asteroid A small rocky or metallic world orbiting the Sun. The Asteroid Belt contains billions of asteroids.

astronomy The science of studying space.

atmosphere The layer of gases around a star, planet or moon.

axis The imaginary line that passes through the poles of a planet and on which the planet spins.

black hole The remains of a star that has collapsed in on itself, with gravity so strong that nothing can escape it.

dark matter The material in the Universe that we cannot see and haven't found yet. It makes up about 95 per cent of the Universe.

galaxy A large number of stars, gas and dust held together by gravity. Our galaxy is the Milky Way.

gravity A force that attracts all objects towards one another.

light-year A unit of measurement based on how far light travels in one year – 9.46 million million km.

lunar To do with the Moon.

mass How much matter there is in an object. Matter is substance that takes up space. It can be solid, liquid, gas or plasma.

moon A natural satellite, orbiting a planet, made of rock or ice.

nebula A cloud of gas and dust where stars are born or have died.

orbit To follow a path around an object in space. Planets orbit stars and moons orbit planets.

probe An uncrewed spacecraft sent to explore other worlds and gather information.

satellite An object in orbit around a planet. Moons are natural satellites. The ISS is an artificial one.

Solar System The Sun and all the objects that orbit it, including the eight or nine planets, at least 175 moons, billions of space rocks and trillions of comets.

star A glowing mass of gas held together by gravity.

supernova A type of exploding star.

Universe Everything that exists – all of space and everything in it.

Further reading and websites

READ MORE ABOUT SPACE:
Knowledge Encyclopedia: Space! (Dorling Kindersley, 2015)

Space: Galaxies and Stars by Ian Graham (Franklin Watts, 2016)

The Story of Astronomy and Space by Louie Stowell
(Usborne Publishing, 2014)

READ MORE ABOUT BEING A GREAT WRITER:
How to Write a Story by Simon Cheshire (Bloomsbury, 2014)

How to Write Your Best Story Ever! by Christopher Edge
(Oxford University Press, 2015)

The Usborne Write Your Own Story Book (Usborne Publishing, 2011)

DISCOVER MORE ABOUT SPACE ONLINE:
www.kidsastronomy.com
Loads of free astronomy resources aimed at children.

www.nasa.gov
The North American Space Agency's official website, which includes
up-to-date news about the International Space Station (ISS).

www.universetoday.com
Website packed with space and astronomy news, plus articles
and pictures about all space phenomena.

Index

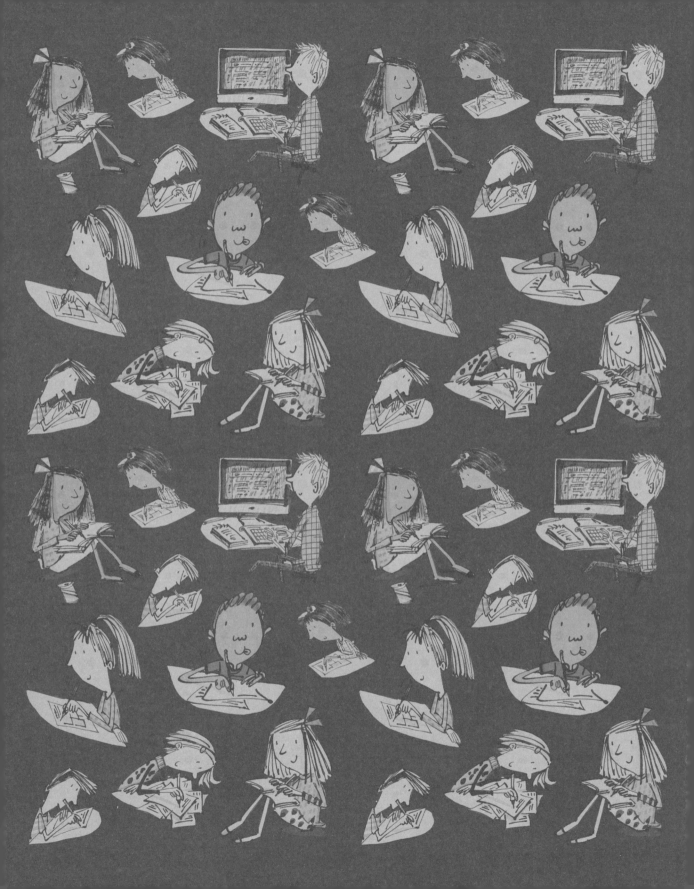

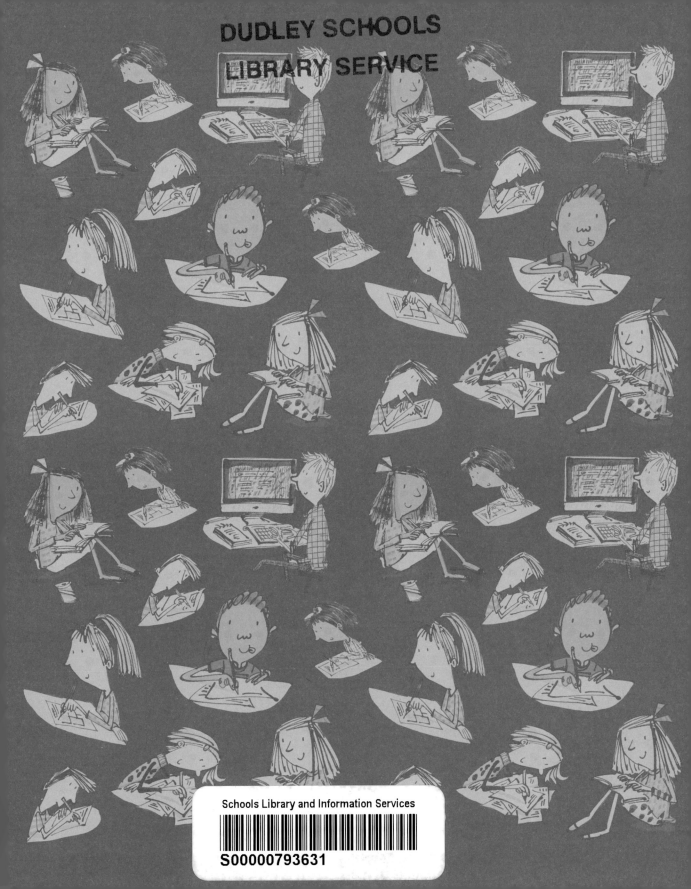